Mindfulness for Beginners

21-Day Step By Step Guide to Relieve Stress and Find Peace in Your Everyday Life

Jill Hesson

© **Copyright 2016 by Jill Hesson - All rights reserved.**

This document is geared towards providing exact and reliable information in regards to the topic and issue covered. The publication is sold with the idea that the publisher is not required to render accounting, officially permitted, or otherwise, qualified services. If advice is necessary, legal or professional, a practiced individual in the profession should be ordered.

- From a Declaration of Principles which was accepted and approved equally by a Committee of the American Bar Association and a Committee of Publishers and Associations.

In no way is it legal to reproduce, duplicate, or transmit any part of this document in either electronic means or in printed format. Recording of this publication is strictly prohibited and any storage of this document is not allowed unless with written permission from the publisher. All rights reserved.

The information provided herein is stated to be truthful and consistent, in that any liability, in terms of inattention or otherwise, by any usage or abuse of any policies, processes, or directions contained within is the solitary and utter responsibility of the recipient reader. Under no circumstances will any legal responsibility or blame be held against the publisher for any reparation, damages, or monetary loss due to the information herein, either directly or indirectly.

Respective authors own all copyrights not held by the publisher.

The information herein is offered for informational purposes solely, and is universal as so. The presentation of the information is without contract or any type of guarantee assurance.

The trademarks that are used are without any consent, and the publication of the trademark is without permission or backing by the trademark owner. All trademarks and brands within this book are for clarifying purposes only and are the owned by the owners themselves, not affiliated with this document.

Table of Contents

Introduction 1

Chapter 1 – Introduction to Mindfulness Days 1-3 3

Chapter 2 – Being Mindful of your Surroundings – Days 4-6 6

Chapter 3 – Learning to Optimize your Meditative Practice – Days 6-10 9

Chapter 4 – Mindful Acceptance – Days 11 to 15 12

Chapter 5 – Exercises in Humility – Days 16 to 18 15

Chapter 6 – Mindfulness of The Wonders Around You – Day 19 and 20 18

Chapter 7 – Day 21 – A Day of Celebration 21

Chapter 8 – What Your Lessons Have Taught You 24

Chapter 9 – The Benefits of Mindfulness 27

Conclusion 30

Introduction

If you have found that life is putting too many strains on you, or that the load that you are left to carry is too heavy, mindfulness may be the answer. People work their minds too hard sometimes. We are taught to think about our actions before we actually put them into practice. We are taught to think before we speak. In today's society, if we had time to relax and enjoy life, it's unlikely that we would, because such are the demands of a modern era. However, when you find out about mindfulness and start to use it, you begin to see things in a very different light. For example, you notice things you didn't notice before. Why? The problem with our philosophy on life is that we tend to look inward instead of seeing what's going on around us.

There are many books on mindfulness and some of them are useful while others seem to be regurgitated information, rather than being of any substance. The difference with this book is that it's written by someone who teaches people to use mindfulness to help improve the quality of their lives. Mindfulness isn't a fad. In fact, it has been taken so seriously by doctors that prescriptions are even being written for students to attend classes to help them to get over the problems associated with stress and anxiety. The success rate is astounding when you compare with traditional treatment using medications. Did you know, for example, that statistics show that in America today, the use of medications for stress related illnesses has increased to a worrying degree but that the figures of people who suffer from anxiety are not going down? Doesn't that tell you something about the efficiency of traditional treatment?

In this book, we look at the possibility of using Mindfulness to be more aware of life, rather than hiding behind medication. Our 21-day step-by-step approach should be sufficient to make you feel less stressed by the end of the 21 days and ready to embrace a fresh approach to anxiety. You won't feel overwhelmed by it. You will feel that you are more in control of your life and you will also feel calmer in demeanor. We would suggest that you follow the steps within the book and try it. You have nothing to lose if you are already stressed to the max and are looking for a solution. Doctors in the United Kingdom have been using Mindfulness to help those suffering with stress because they have recognized that there is little benefit in stifling people with medications that cause patients to be trapped in a vicious cycle. I am depressed – Take anti-depressants – Hide behind the drugs so that you don't have to face the world or the reasons for your unhappiness. Now look at what Mindfulness does. I am depressed though willing to seek out solutions to make my life better, and will use Mindfulness to achieve inner peace and happiness. I know which way you would rather go.

Chapter 1 – Introduction to Mindfulness Days 1-3

"If you want to conquer the anxiety of life, live in the moment. Live in the breath" ~ Amit Ray

If you are on medication for anxiety related illnesses, it is not suggested that you come off these medications without any kind of medical supervision, but you can start to introduce mindfulness into your life – even when you are taking these medications. The problem with taking medications is that you can't just go "cold turkey" and should not put your body through this kind of treatment. We suggest that you follow the steps shown in this book and when you feel a lot stronger, you can approach your medical professional and adjust your medication, so that you take control of your life.

Day one to three

Step 1 – Learning how your subconscious mind works

Your mind is programmed by the life that you live. All the time, your subconscious mind records all of your responses to stimuli. The subconscious doesn't deal with things such as emotions. If you are afraid of snakes and see one, your mind will know that the right way for you to react is to be afraid. Therapists who deal with anxiety such as this usually suggest introducing stimuli in small controlled doses until your mind is able to feel more comfortable with that particular thing. However, life works that way as well. When you are angry, for example, your subconscious recognizes the thing that made you angry. The next time that thing happens, you will be angry again.

However, you can change the pattern of events because if you show your subconscious mind another reaction to those stimuli, it will relearn your pattern of behavior and will not expect you to get angry given the same circumstances – once your mind is trained. The reason mindfulness is so useful is because it empties out preconceptions. You are told to empty the mind of thought and that's contrary to everything we know about reacting. Your subconscious has much more time to work because it's not crowded out with thoughts – either negative or positive – and is able to help you to see things in a much clearer light.

One of the stumbling blocks that people come across that stops them from being positive is that they don't know how to relax. In this step, we teach you to relax as it forms a very important part of mindfulness. When you meditate, for example, you are mindful of your breathing. The trouble with this advice is that most people don't know how to breathe properly. They assume that air going in and out of the body is sufficient to sustain life, but they don't see it as more than that.

Relaxation and Breathing

We have spread this step over three days because you cannot undo the habits of a lifetime in less. You need to:

- Learn to relax
- Learn to empty the mind
- Learn to let go
- Learn to breathe correctly

You can do this over a three-day period. Thus, on the first day you learn the basics and on the second and third days, you put the theory into practice. It will take you half an hour each day for the next three days.

Exercise in relaxation and breathing

Be dressed in comfortable clothing and lie on the bed, using one pillow to support your head. Your arms should be at your sides and your legs straight. Start to learn to breathe correctly. Inhale through the nostrils to the count of 7, hold the breath for the count of 3 and then breathe out. Now, place your hand on your upper abdomen. Do the breathing again in the same way and feel your upper abdomen pivot. Adjust your breathing until it does and then breathe in and out and concentrate solely on your breathing. If thoughts come into your mind, you need to acknowledge them and then just let go of them. Go back to the beginning again, concentrating solely on your breathing. Then work through feeling each part of the body. Close your eyes. Think of your toes. Tense them and then let them go so that they are relaxed, breathing in the same way as we showed you all the way through feeling a part of your body and tensing it and then relaxing it until you have worked all the way up your body and have reached the top of your head. For the next three days, put aside time to do this exercise. It is only a small exercise, but it is one big leap away from stress and will help you with later exercises.

Chapter 2 – Being Mindful of your Surroundings – Days 4-6

"Looking at the beauty of the world is the first step to purifying the mind" ~ Amit Ray

Being aware of what is going on in your own surroundings helps you to be more accepting of life. Over the course of the next three days, we are going to observe life and at the same time, learn acceptance of the part that you play in your life. During the exercises on these three days, you will be asked to follow the instructions well because they will help you to see how much you are missing in life and how you can change the way you react to the world around you and the people in it.

Exercise in self-control

In the next three days, we want you to change from being reactive to being accepting. Each time someone says something to you, which would normally spark the reaction of anger, or any other negative feeling in your mind, I want you to accept what was said, acknowledge it and then let it go. The problem with people is that they allow their emotions to react in negative ways and this builds up a lot of resentment and unhappiness. Letting go is so important. The habits that brought you here to learn about mindfulness have meant that your life is stressed. It's time to let go. Respond to people with a positive statement. For example, if someone says something that makes you mad, they are looking for a reaction. They type of reaction you give determines the peace of mind that you experience. If you merely acknowledge it and move on, you don't allow the negativity to get through to you. Try to control how you react so that during the course of the next three days, you only react to the world with positivity. It will be hard at first, but you are learning to be mindful of your responses and also learning to let go of the very thing that is harming you – negativity.

Let's give you an example. Someone says something to wind you up. Greet it with a smile. Dismiss the thought and move onto the next thought. The less you are able to look back at that thought and analyze it in your head, the better you will be. The catchphrase you need to remember is that what is past is past. Now is the beginning.

Exercise in observation

Do you have a favorite place near where you live? If you do, go there and learn to take in the scenery and use this to inspire you. I remember a place that I used to use when I was new to mindfulness. It was a hill that overlooked moorland on all sides and that was a wonderful place to go at sunrise or sunset because the colors were so amazing. In that place, you get to realize how small you are and that's a good thing. It helps you to be humble and humility is the cornerstone to happiness. You can look for miles and realize how small you are in comparison with everything. You may even see yourself as a grain of sand or a pebble on a distant shore, but you have to also appreciate that without all those grains of sand and pebbles, there would be no beach. Therefore, even though you are small, the role that you play in your life is vitally important to your surroundings and to how others see you and how you see yourself.

When you go to your chosen place, practice the breathing exercise that I showed you in the last chapter, but this time sit up straight and hold your back straight. Throughout the body, we have something called Chakras or energy centers. When people are stressed, these can get blocked. By sitting straight when you breathe and meditate, you open up the energy centers and allow energy to flow through your body and that's extremely important.

Observe the scenery. Notice everything. Look at the color of the leaves, the sky and the clouds and take a little time to think of nothing else. This moment could be the most important in your life because you may suddenly realize how wonderful nature is and how relaxed it can make you feel. Often people who spend time in natural surroundings feel calmer and those who have pets often extol the therapeutic value of having a pet because it's letting nature into their homes and it takes away some of the negativity in your life when you do spend any time with nature.

Using the senses

Mindfulness is all about being aware of your senses and using them to make the tapestry of your life richer. Instead of simply eating your food without really enjoying it, savor the aroma, let the food sit on your tongue and make the most of your sense of taste. Then when you chew your food, chew it well and enjoy all the sensations of crunchiness or softness of the different kinds of textures your food consists of. When listening to the world, make the most of your ears. Hear the children laughing. Hear the birds singing. Instead of taking your world for granted, start to feel it through the senses because that's what people in these modern times have forgotten to do.

Chapter 3 – Learning to Optimize your Meditative Practice – Days 6-10

"Everything is created twice, first in the mind and then in reality." ~ Robin S. Sharma

There is so much that goes on in the mind over the course of a day. Even when sleeping, things are happening in the mind. Those who are stressed find that the mind takes over and instead of looking outward and getting inspiration from life, those suffering from stress or anxiety tend to look inward and they don't find the inspiration that they need because their thought patterns are negative. Although, in this day and age, medications are used to raise the levels of serotonin to make people happier, you can do it yourself using mindfulness and it's quite easy even for those who have never tried it before.

Over the next four days, your task is to set up a space in your home for meditation. This should contain things such as a stool or cushion to sit on and inspirational things that you enjoy, such as candles, incense sticks, a Buddha statue and pictures that inspire you. Remember that you are not worshipping a Buddha statue so if the idea conflicts with your religion, you need to understand that statues in Buddhism are not Gods. They are simply inspirational items to help those who want to meditate to feel calm and relaxed. Thus, there is no conflict whatsoever with your own given religion. Often people have the misconception that anything touching on Buddhism is religious, when in fact it isn't. It is philosophical or related to a way of life.

The place that you choose should be sufficient comfortable with no real distractions such as TV noise or people walking past. Try to find somewhere that you can devote to meditation because meditation should become a daily event, even if you can only spare about three quarters of an hour. In the initial stages of meditation, you will only need half an hour but you will find that your own mind will know when you need a longer time to meditate and enjoy the practice.

Meditation in Mindfulness Practice

This takes on different guises but for the sake of introduction, I will talk about the kind of meditation that will help you to improve your life. You need to be dressed in clothing that is comfortable and sit on your stool or cushion with your ankles crossed. You don't need to try complex positions such as the full lotus because these positions are for the more experienced practitioner.

Simply cross your ankles and place your hands in the following position. Your main hand (if you are right handed, this will be your right hand) should be placed on your lap palm facing upward and your left hand on top in a similar position. Your thumbs should touch each other. This keeps you from fiddling around when you are meditating and helps to ground you so that you are able to concentrate in a more efficient way. It is vital that your back is straight. Your head should look directly in front of you so that your airways are free to breathe. I generally get students to sway a little on their backside until they have found the perfect balance in the sitting position as this helps you to keep still while you meditate.

Meditative Breathing

Just like you did before, you breathe in through the nose to the count of seven and then hold the breath for a few minutes before breathing out to the count of eight. Think of the airflow as being something solid that you can see. Most people imagine it like flames of fire going into the body and then leaving. The reason you need to visualize the breathing process as a tangible thing rather than trying to concentrate on something that you cannot see. Breathe in – hold it – breathe out several times until you feel a rhythm develop. Then you are ready to meditate. You need to bear in mind that the only thing that should go through your mind while you meditate is the breath itself. If you find that your mind wanders – and it always does – acknowledge the thought and then go back to your meditation. Don't worry about it as it happens to all beginners.

When you are ready to meditate, start as follows:

- Close your eyes
- Breathe in through the nostrils – count 7
- Hold the breath – count 3
- Let the breath out – count 8

Keeping your eyes closed continue to use the breathing shown in the last three sentences and each time that you breathe out count. You will start with one when you have done it once and through to ten. The idea is to aim at getting to ten without thoughts creeping into your head at all. If they do, go back to one again and start over.

Over the course of the next four days, pick a time every day to practice your meditation. It is something you need to develop into a habit. You should meditate every day to get better at doing it and to optimize the experience. Therefore, getting into a daily routine now will help you to keep this as part of your life.

Chapter 4 – Mindful Acceptance – Days 11 to 15

"Be happy in the moment. That's enough. Each moment is all we need, not more" ~ Mother Teresa

People have all kinds of expectations about what happiness is. They think that it is a perpetual feeling of contentment. In this day and age, people try to find it through being rich or by spending money or even by taking great vacations, but at the end of all of these activities, they are disappointed to find that these are temporary things that don't buy any kind of substance. Thus, happiness can only be achieved when you are able to accept who you are in the moment that you are in. Too many people look back in their lives and allow their baggage to become that they are. The past is gone. Sure, you may have a few remaining emotional hurdles to get over because of the past, but these hurdles can be put to one side when you learn mindfulness. This takes you out of the past and into this very moment that you are in. The exercises you will do over the next 5 days are important to the development of your mind. They will help you to accept yourself and they will also help you to drop negative values.

Exercise in thought control

If you had full control over your thought processes, you could eliminate negativity, for example, and this would contribute to happiness. However, life isn't as simplistic as that. You first need to learn to clear out all the clutter. If you have been depressed or have suffered from anxiety in your life, this is hard to drop. However, when you learn to discipline your mind, you take control over how you see things. You are also able to acknowledge and dismiss those things that do not add value to your life. This exercise is going to be one of the hardest exercises for you to do because it won't seem natural at first. You are accustomed to having a mind filled with thoughts and it's not easy to get rid of that habit. What we need you to do is to find a very quiet place to sit down. When you are seated, we need you to close your eyes and to try to think of absolutely nothing. You are going to find it a struggle. Every time thoughts creep in, just dismiss them and then go back to thinking of nothing. You need to do this for about 10 minutes every day because it's helping you to train your mind into being able to dismiss things when they do not add any value to your life.

Second part of thought control exercise

Now that you have emptied your mind of thought, open your eyes and observe everything that you see around you. Instead of allowing your thoughts to wander into things that are not happening in this moment in time, concentrate all of your thoughts upon what surrounds you. Typical thoughts could be:

I am in a room that is warm and tidy. There are rugs on the floor and the light is shining into the room. There is a fireplace and upon it, there are blue and white Chinese vases. If I look across the room, there are bonsai plants in the right hand corner of the room and looking out of the windows, the sky is gray and the trees are losing their leaves. I can see that the air outside is cold and I can also see birds flying down to take food from the feeder that I have placed in the garden.

What you are learning by doing this is to live in the moment but to add no judgement to what you see. I didn't say if I liked the blue and white vases. I didn't say if it pleased me that it was fall. I didn't say what my emotions were about the place I am in. All I did was look around me and describe what I saw without any form of judgement and that's what you need to do. The kind of things you should not be saying to yourself, for example:

I must tidy up this room. There is dust on the dresser and it looks a mess. I forgot to dust the light shades and the spider's web in the corner needs sorting out.

The difference between these and the initial thoughts is that these are judgmental. They make me feel bad because I haven't done what I should have done, but they are also negative thoughts. One can observe things that need doing, but the moment that you place judgement into the picture, you turn your thoughts into negative thoughts and that's the mistake that many people make. All of these negative and judgmental thoughts add up and cause stress or anxiety, so it's important to see the difference and to practice every day observing the world in the here and now without judging yourself so harshly. On these days, allow yourself time to reflect on your moments as they pass and instead of making those moments burdens of the past or worries about the future, be in the moment. Enjoy them and learn to see the brightness even in small things that may at first seem negative. During my exercise of this for this book, I actually saw a spider creating his web on one of the bushes in the garden and it was a wonderful sight to behold. The trouble with our lives is that we are too busy planning or regretting and do not actually take the time needed to appreciate the moment that we are in. Start living and start enjoying the moment. Stop judging it because the moment you do, you introduce the potential of stress.

Chapter 5 – Exercises in Humility – Days 16 to 18

"True humility is not thinking less of yourself; it is thinking of yourself less." ~ C. S. Lewis

I love the above quotation because it's so clever. We center our lives around ourselves as this is the natural thing for a human being to do, but all the time that we spend thinking of ourselves is time wasted. Not only that but it fires up the imagination and allows it to conjure up all kinds of negative thoughts and to harbor grudges for things that have gone by. Mindfulness doesn't do that, and the exercises in this chapter for days 16 through to 18 are something that any human being will gain from – they are exercises in humility.

Steps to learn a humble approach

Why does having a humble approach matter? If you have high expectations of others or of yourself and you don't live up to those expectations, you set yourself up for disappointment. However, if you approach life with humility and mindfulness at the same time, you don't. Let's take a look over the next few days at how humility is tackled when you are in a retreat or learning how to introduce mindfulness into the way that you live. In a retreat, you may be given mundane work to do that you feel is boring. It may be that the work is servile in nature. Perhaps you will be asked to peel potatoes or clean floors. I remember being asked to do this and my guru taught me that you approach each task in life with the same enthusiasm and the same amount of determination. You may not have an end goal in sight but you use these tasks to develop the way that you think. Thus, in this chapter, we are dealing with how to get through the mundane and retain the right attitude so that humility is top in your list of qualities.

Choose a task – Everyone has tasks that are mundane. For me, it's cleaning floors. For a man, it may be cleaning the car. There are many such tasks in life that we put aside for other things. It may be cleaning the ring mark from the bath or scrubbing the toilet. Whatever that task is, it should be a routine one that betters the quality of your life. Choose a task that you don't usually like performing. Approach the task with the right tools. While you are doing the task, think of nothing except the task that you are concentrating on. If you find your thoughts wandering, accept the interruption and then dismiss it, going back to the task at hand. Concentrate totally on the task and make sure that you do your best to not only do it, but to do it well. Be sufficiently happy that you have performed this task and think nothing negative about it. See it for what it is. It's an exercise in humility.

While you perform the task, concentrate on every aspect of it. For example, while you are washing a floor, note how the clean area looks so much better than grimy areas. Note how much your scrubbing improves the surface of the floor. Think of nothing else. Be in that moment and give it everything that you are.

The reason that humility works is because it helps you to become less shallow. You stop sweating the small stuff and begin to see life as it really is. If you can use this exercise on your daily chores and immerse yourself in them, you are less likely to let negative thoughts fester in your mind. Put them aside and simply give the task all that you are. For those who are not sure which tasks are good for this, there is a list below of potential jobs that can help you to get back to basics and forget your thoughts about the past or worries about the future:

- Car washing
- Floor washing
- Weeding between vegetable plants
- Sweeping the floor
- Washing the dishes
- Getting rid of cobwebs

Whichever jobs you choose to do, make sure that you approach the jobs with a good heart and a positive attitude without thinking of the job as being onerous. Everyone has to do jobs in their lives but many use this time to think bad thoughts. For example, a woman who is having difficulty with her husband may be thinking about the relationship while doing menial tasks and what that does is make the problems worse. Thus, by preventing thought about other things and keeping your breathing at a reasonable rhythm, you are able to allow your subconscious mind a little bit of time to work out things that your conscious mind may be too busy or too filled up to handle.

I cannot stress enough how important humility is. It helps you to make the most of whom you are and mindfulness depends upon having a humble approach. Thus for these 3 days, practice putting humility into tasks that you know you have to do, and continue with that attitude after those days are finished.

Chapter 6 – Mindfulness of The Wonders Around You – Day 19 and 20

"Looking at beauty in the world is the first step to purifying the mind" ~ Amit Ray

The next steps are going to seem rather easy compared with what you have learned so far. Every day, in your life, you go through the routines of going to work or looking after the home and you may be stuck in traffic or you may find that there are times when you are overwhelmed by all the duties that you have to perform in the space of a day. Well, we are going to try and change that for you. The pattern I have chosen to introduce mindfulness from the moment that you get up in the morning should help you to see the world in a different light.

Step 1 – Day 19 Breakfast

You know that you need to be up at a certain time to have your breakfast. On these days, if you need to set the alarm clock a little earlier in order to achieve time to sit and enjoy your breakfast with your family, then do so. It is important that you start your day with the fresh aroma of breakfast at a leisurely pace. Enjoy every taste, every flavor and every texture. Enjoy your coffee and take your time eating. This is very important because people who are nervous tend to eat quickly and the main part of your body that suffers when you are nervous or anxious is your stomach. Today you will be conscious of your stomach and take care of its needs.

Step 2 – Being aware of what's around you

As you go to work, look at what's around you. Instead of rushing, take your time and look at the natural elements that you pass on the way to work. For example, are the trees losing their leaves? Are there flowers in bloom? What color is the sky? ==Be in the moment. Stop losing parts of your life because you are thinking of other things==. Be aware that people you work with may also have their own personal issues. If people are not as nice as you wish they would be, be kind and empathize. If you are negative, you add to your own stress and you add to theirs.

Step 3 – Lunch

When taking time for lunch, make sure that you choose something nutritious that won't make you lethargic in the afternoon. A light and nutritious lunch can be enjoyed in the same way as you enjoyed your breakfast. Be there, taste every taste and appreciate it and try to think only of your food and the enjoyment of the meal. If you cannot have a full lunch, take your sandwiches to the park and appreciate your surroundings. You need that break away from work so eating sandwiches on the go or at your desk doesn't achieve the same thing. Allow yourself to have contact with nature and you will be able to take your time eating and really appreciate each taste. Observe the world and what's happening in that particular moment without worrying about the afternoon or anything that lies ahead. You need to be in the moment.

Step 4 – Avoiding Stress

During your afternoons, take work as it comes. Relax about the amount you have and concentrate on each job as it happens instead of letting your mind wander elsewhere. You will achieve more if you do not multi task, but stay grounded in the moment. Turn off distractions and allow yourself to absorb your work and enjoy it. Avoid all kinds of conflict with others. Be kind and courteous. That way, when the end of the day comes, you are not in an anxious state that makes your evening with your family difficult. Go home, switch off and prepare the evening meal with a smile on your face. The thing that people do is take their work problems home and that eats into family time. Remember that what has happened is finished and what hasn't yet happened isn't worth worrying about. Be in the moment.

Step 5 – Arranging your meditation sessions

These should be at least two hours from meals, so that you are not suffering from indigestion while trying to meditate. Space your evening so that you have time to give to loved ones and enjoy their company. The time that is needed for meditation isn't actually long but it's important and should be done on a daily basis. When you switch off to do your meditation, don't bring problems with you. People in your family need to appreciate that this time is spent on something that helps you to cope and to be happy and they should respect your time alone.

Chapter 7 – Day 21 – A Day of Celebration

"Mind is a flexible mirror. Adjust it to see a better world."
~Amit Ray

If you have been through all of the exercises contained in this book so far, you are right on track. You will be able to see for yourself the positive influence that mindfulness has on your life. You no longer think about all the negative things that you used to have in your mind. You no longer see everything from a negative viewpoint and your mental health will be better. This is the last day of learning. After this, you need to keep to a routine where mindfulness is part of your life, every day that you live because when it is, you adjust the way that you look at life and can overcome much of the difficulty that life throws your way.

You will have learned to let go of negative feelings. You will also have learned that each moment holds new promise for you. Today's exercise is an exercise in letting go. Take a piece of paper and a pen and be ready to let go of problems that may have been bugging you because they hold you back in your life and it's only because of the way you look at life that these problems exist. For example, Jill told me that her problems were because of her boyfriend's attitude at the beginning of her mindfulness practice. By the end of the exercises I have given to you, she was able to discern that HE wasn't the problem. The problem was that SHE was seeing things in a negative manner. She blamed him, but he wasn't to blame. When she changed her attitude toward him, she became much more positive and interacted with his friends in an easier manner and actually found that she became a better person for letting go of negative thoughts. They were unfounded anyway but we all have thoughts that hold us back.

Write down the first negative thought that comes into your mind. Don't try too hard. Simply write it down and recognize it as being harmful to your happiness. Write down another and another. Use post it notes if you want to or separate sheets of paper. Then meditate for 20 minutes. Hold each of the pieces of paper in your hands after your meditation and read what you wrote. You may, for example, have written:

I am not very good with people

See the words. They are in this moment because you placed them there. No, rip up the piece of paper and dismiss the thought. Letting go of negativity after meditation is usually quite successful because your mind is already relaxed and happy and your subconscious mind gets the right message instead of the wrong one. A negative influence – i.e. the piece of paper – comes into your moment. You acknowledge it; you dismiss it and you tear up the paper symbolically to let your mind know that you have been able to let go. If you find any of these thoughts coming to your mind from now on, dismiss them instantly and think of something else. You may use concentration on your breathing to get you past that moment or you can concentrate on a thing.

For example, if you have something in the room that is inspirational, concentrate on that instead of concentrating on the negative. Let go and you will find that it is habit forming and once you are able to let go, the habit you are creating is a much more positive one that will make you happier in the moment you find yourself in. The same can be done if, for example, you wake up from a bad dream. Concentrate on something in your room or on your breathing and allow the bad thoughts to go away. They will if you banish them and you have power over what amount of negativity you allow into your life.

When you are able to do this, you will be able to meditate with your eyes open and be aware of beautiful things around you. Try to meditate by the sea, or even in your favorite place but while you are meditating, try to concentrate on one particular focal point. For example, in your home, this could be a candle. Think of the candle and look at it. See the flame but do not let your thoughts wander to other things. The celebration is not having to close your eyes to actually switch off those thought processes, but not letting the things around you fill your mind with pointless rubbish. Your mind is as free as you wish it to be and you can meditate even on a packed airplane if you want to.

Celebrate life by making sure that you use your senses to the utmost every day and every minute of your life. Taste your food; take your time to enjoy the tastes and the textures. Take your time eating it. Allow your senses to enjoy everything about your life. You can open the curtains in the morning and actually smell the season. I remember thinking how wonderful it was to smell the optimism in the air in spring or the still of the world in winter. Enjoy it by being in the moment because that's what mindfulness is all about. The Dalai Lama commented once that what he thought of the way mankind lived their lives was a little strange. They spend all of their time trying to chase after the dream of money, and make themselves ill doing it. Then they spend all of the money they earn on medical bills so that they can feel better. The problem, as he saw it, was that they go through life worrying about tomorrow or looking back on yesterday and never actually get to live their lives in the moment and by the time that they do, it's too late.

Incorporate all of these lessons into your life and it becomes a much less anxious place.

Chapter 8 – What Your Lessons Have Taught You

"In this moment, there is plenty of time. In this moment, you are precisely where you should be. In this moment, there is infinite possibility." ~ Victoria Moran

During the course of this book, we have mentioned the qualities of mindfulness and humility but there are things that people allow into their lives that are negative and during the course of your life, one of the most difficult things to do is to forgive. Without forgiveness, human beings have something missing from their lives and that is compassion. When you do not feel compassion for people who do things that you consider as wrong, you miss out on the possibility of living your life to the full.

Over the course of your lifetime, you are presented with opportunities to shine and many do not live up to that possibility taking their regrets with them each step of the way. You may be among those people but you do need to know that mindfulness doesn't have room for bitterness and regret. Yes, of course, there are periods of your life, which sadden you, but today is the first day toward the rest of your life. You need to let go of all kinds of bad feelings because these all contribute to the unhappiness or stress that you feel. Let me give you an example.

Clair felt very unhappy because her husband was unfaithful. The doubts that she had followed her for years but they did her no service at all. She didn't trust life. She didn't trust anyone in her life and she had very little self-confidence. If she had analyzed the situation correctly, she would have known that she and her husband were not a good match in the first place. He criticized who she was and she felt smaller than she should have felt. In feeling small, she harbored so much baggage from that relationship that she dragged it into every aspect of her life, until she became very small and insignificant.

When she discovered mindfulness, it was very hard for her to let go of all of this baggage, even though it had happened years ago. I talked her through the process of letting go and she would almost reach it, but there was a part of her clinging onto that relationship to such an extent that she found it almost impossible to let go. Another person who did the same thing was Elizabeth Gilbert in her book, Eat, Pray, Love, but when both of these women did eventually let go, they found that it was easier than they thought.

They were trying too hard to let go and consciously seeing the process, got to the stage where they were actually too frightened to let go, knowing that both of them had never had to step out of what they saw as their "comfort" zone. They were familiar with suffering. Without suffering, they didn't know what lay ahead. If you can imagine a river with stepping stones, both of these women and indeed many others stay on one stone and do not move forward because fear stops them. They are defined by their misery and are frightened to let go of it and step into unfamiliar territory. Both Clair and Elizabeth finally did take that leap of faith and found that it wasn't as frightening as they thought it would be. They were able to forgive and to move on and as soon as they did, their lives improved. They were able to mend themselves and become whole characters and lost the inferiority complex along the way.

While you continue to live in the past, you deny yourself of a future. You need to simply acknowledge that you had the thought and then let it go, just as you would let go of the strings of a balloon and see it floating into the horizon. That's the hardest thing for anxious people to do, but actually one of the easiest. It's hard to imagine because you have never taken yourself there, but when you do, you begin to see how simply it is and wonder why you didn't let go earlier.

The kind of things that you need to let go of are:

- Jealousy
- Hate
- Negativity
- Lack of belief in yourself
- Lack of belief in others

If your attitude is always sarcastic, you may need to let go of that too because it may be that which is holding you back and making your life less happy than it needs to be.

Mindfulness will help you to do all of that, but it does a lot more as well. In the next chapter, we will talk about the benefits of all of this practice. When you know what you can gain from it, you will grab the potential with both hands and will find that stress and strain will disappear from your life and that you find a peace and calm you never thought possible.

Chapter 9 – The Benefits of Mindfulness

"Life is a dance. Mindfulness is witnessing that dance." ~ Amit Ray

A very long time before the birth of Christ, there was a young prince who was relatively protected from the world by his parents. They did not want him to see how much suffering existed in the world outside of his castle. However, the prince was curious about the world and wandered out into it and saw human suffering first hand. It troubled him and he wanted to know why human beings have to go through such suffering. Siddhartha Gautama dedicated his life to finding out what mankind could do to lessen the suffering that they had to endure and what he came up with is still used today to improve the lives of people who are troubled. He found that much of the suffering comes from the actual actions of people themselves. Mindfulness is part and parcel of the Eightfold Path that was designed within Buddhist philosophy to improve the lives of those who chose to take this path. The path led to enlightenment for some, but improved the lives of those who followed it. It included such things as:

- Right action
- Right speech
- Right attitude
- Right Mindfulness
- Right work

And the list of things that Siddhartha Gautama attributed to sadness and suffering helped people to step beyond that suffering and made them stronger. Mindfulness, as we know it today, is based upon the premise that if people act in the right way and say the right things, have the right attitude and are mindful, their lives will improve. It's not just an improvement in who you are. It goes beyond that. The improvement permeates through to the health that you suffer and the happiness that you find within your life.

Let's look at the health benefits of mindfulness. Your heartbeat goes down when you meditate and your blood pressure decreases as well, but it doesn't just happen when you meditate. What happens is that you become a calmer person. You begin to be able to look at life in a much simpler fashion and don't have to take all the baggage from the past with you through every day of your life. You appreciate things more and find that your body improves as a consequence of this. You don't suffer anxiety and your overall health is strengthened by the fact that mindfulness is part and parcel of your life.

What doctors in the United Kingdom have found is that instead of prescribing medications, they are actually prescribing mindfulness courses for people who have anxiety disorders and depression and that people are gaining so much more from it than they ever did from pills.

There are discourses between scientists and the Dalai Lama and there's a book that perhaps you can read to help you develop your personality so that you can clearly see that mindfulness is able to do what science is not. It is able to help you to make fundamental changes to your approach in life, which helps you, in turn, to put away negativity and to become stronger. You find that with forgiveness, you are able to move through each day and see it as a new opportunity. You don't hold onto the negativity of the past and are able to free up your mind to seeing life in a different way. Imagine the brain as being packed with boxes. These boxes are all the experiences that you have in life. Unfortunately, most people hold onto elements of the past so that there's no room for now. When you are able to learn to let go, you empty out those boxes and allow your subconscious mind to see a very different approach to life.

As we said earlier in the book, the subconscious mind actually records your life and your reactions to given stimuli. If you always shake when you meet new people, then the subconscious will trigger that action. However, if you are able to observe and then let go and make this a habit, your subconscious information can be rewritten so that panic is not your automatic response to being presented with new situations. Whenever you get into thoughts that are uncomfortable about the past, let them go. There's nothing to say that they have to take over your life to such an extent that they stop you from living in the present and that's the mistake that anxious people make. Mindfulness and meditation help you to still the mind and when you start to do that, you begin to see that life isn't as complex and complicated as you previously made it.

Of course, during the course of a lifetime, negative things will happen. Friends die or disappointing things happen, but then you move on. You have a choice to move on with positive thoughts of those who have gone – which is healthy – or harbor negative thoughts that make you less of a person. Mindfulness makes you stronger and thus you are more capable of dealing with bad things, so you don't have to carry them with you as baggage. Instead, you see them as lessons in life, learn from them and then move forward. By doing this, you are not being disrespectful but you are learning a new acceptance of life that allows you to be stronger, more compassionate and be able to empathize genuinely when the need arises.

Conclusion

Throughout this book, we have appreciated that you are new to mindfulness and that until you read this book, you didn't have much idea about what mindfulness was. I have made the lessons relatively easy and although you will experience difficulty at first getting your head around stillness, you will eventually realize that it is this stillness within your mind that helps to make you stronger. You will also appreciate that life is much richer when you can move through it, one moment at a time. When I started to write this book, the sun was coming through the window and the skies were blue. As I have progressed in the writing, the weather has changed, but I have not kept the image of blue skies in my mind because that wouldn't be real. What is real is that the skies outside my house at this very moment in time are gray and threatening rain. Similarly, you can't drag all of your emotional baggage from one moment to the next unless you want to suffer. Letting go is easier than you may imagine and the first steps toward it are contained within the pages of this book.

Go back through the 21-day course and if you have not managed to become more mindful, try it again because now you have better insight into what it takes, and you are capable of doing this at any time you wish to. Within the pages of this book are all the facts that you need to know about mindfulness though you will find that eventually, this develops into something very special. I have not really gone into what "enlightenment" is because it can frighten people who are unaccustomed to that feeling. Enlightenment and spirituality will come as something that follows if you keep to the routine of meditation and mindfulness. It's almost like a waking up of the mind. Stress becomes a part of the past because you don't need it and it doesn't enhance your life in the slightest. Anxiety disappears because you are breathing in the right way and are not over-oxygenating your body because of anxious breathing habits. You learn to respect your posture and learn that the energy centers in your body allow full flow when you do. You also learn something crucial to your happiness and completeness. You learn who you are in relation to the world around you and see yourself as the person who you want to be.

You are compassionate. You are able to forgive. You are also capable of stepping from one moment into the next with a calmness that you never thought possible. How do I know this? The fact is that I took the same journey as you a very long time ago and what I found along the way was that I do have an enlightened sense of what life is all about and who I am. I am not important, nor do I inflate my opinion of myself but I am able to go into each moment of my life with the expectation that I will be able to cope and change and even enjoy what life has in store for me. When I know that there are going to be troubled waters, I don't dread them anymore. I don't hide away from them. I simply accept the good with the bad and find that life is kinder than it is cruel. Of course, there are troubled waters occasionally, but they are not of my making and that makes it much easier for me to handle and to let go of.

When you go through life using mindfulness as your philosophy, you do so with an open heart. You are able to take the bad with the good and the enlightenment is simply knowing that whatever life throws at you, you are ready to take that moment and enjoy it to the best of your ability – not letting the past doubts creep in or the worries for the future. When you feel that way, you gain a new sense of confidence and are able to love your life and share happiness with others. You may not like everybody. That's natural, but you can empathize with them or put yourself in their shoes and see things in a very different way. That person who made your life difficult didn't actually do that. YOU made your life difficult by perceiving problems. Let them go and the problem is no longer there. They are of YOUR making. That's one of the hardest lessons of all to learn. YOU control your life. If you are ill, there are chances that you contributed to it. Be mindful in your treatment of your body and many things improve. Of course there are illnesses you can do nothing about because they are genetic or because they are things that happen, but you can keep yourself generally in good shape by eating the right things and taking your time doing it. Your body needs good nutrition, exercise and attention to posture, and when you open up all the channels of energy throughout your body, you feel better in yourself.

I hope that this guide has helped you to see that mindfulness really can improve your life and that the 21 days allotted to introducing this will have served you well. There are different books with different approaches, but the reason mine is ordered in the way I have written it is because I have been where you are standing and know the skepticism with which you will approach this new way of looking at life. That's okay. It's normal. You don't change the way you approach life overnight, but it's very possible to do and not only that, it's easier than you anticipate. You will come across problems along the way. For example, emptying your mind and thinking of nothing isn't that easy. That's why we introduced concentration on your breathing. That way, you have something to fill the gap in your thought processes as you meditate. People often say that they don't feel anything during meditation, but the purpose of meditation isn't to feel anything. It's to close down all of the thought processes and make your mind stronger. It also helps your body because human beings, in this day and age, don't allow themselves that "me" time that they need. Try to respect the idea of meditating on a daily basis and you will begin to reap the benefits and see a difference in your approach to life.

I have purposely made the instructions clear enough for someone with absolutely no experience in Buddhism because the information in the book is aimed at everyone. As we have already said, Buddhist ways are not a religion. They are a philosophy. The other thing to remember is something that was said by the Dalai Lama about it being our duty to spread happiness. That's not idealistic and doesn't involve smiles in all the wrong places. That just means being able to satisfy our lives by not inflicting harm on people around us. When people can depend upon you for your wisdom and the fact that you are able to offer something positive to life, you find you actually draw people to you. You also learn which of these people are toxic to your life and eliminate them from your way of thinking. There will always be critiques and that's fine as long as mindfulness allows you to let go of any negativity they may try to pass on to you.

The biggest message of the book is that you can indeed drop all of your negative traits and embrace positive ones and allow your life to continue so that you are no longer living in the past or living with other people's regrets. You are yourself and as an individual are entitled to enjoy the moments your life presents to you. If you walk away from this possibility, you may be dogged for years by the negative values that you hold dear. If you want to step beyond those negative values, read the book again and change your approach to life. You will find that the value your life gives you is so much more than you ever thought possible when you do.

Finally, if you enjoyed this book, then I'd like to ask you for a favor, would you be kind enough to leave a review for this book on Amazon? It'd be greatly appreciated!

Click here to leave a review for this book on Amazon!

https://goo.gl/FHXOhN

Thank you and good luck!

Preview Of
'Yoga: 4-Week Step By Step Guide for Yoga Beginners'

Introduction

We live in a world where we feel completely lost and just riding along. We feel as if we just exist without any particular purpose in life. When that happens, anxiousness, stress and depression starts creeping in, and we stop taking care of how we look as well as our health. The result is an unhealthy lifestyle, which may even advance to various health complications. Have you gotten to that point of your life where you feel you need to find your purpose and bring order to your currently disorderly life?

Well, yoga can do all that since it can help you to bring the much needed order in your physical, mental and spiritual life. What do you think yoga is? Do you think of it as simply executing Olympics level gymnastics stunts? Well, yoga is much more than these stunts. This book will introduce you to yoga, what it is all about and how you can start practicing yoga in as little as 4 weeks.

The Basics

"Yoga" is a Sanskrit word formed from a Latin word *'yoke'* meaning to join. From a human perspective, the easiest way to understand yoga is to view it as a union of various aspects of the human spirit and body such as the physical, mental, and spiritual being.

In simpler language, we can define yoga as spiritual techniques and exercises that are designed to 'join' your body and mind. It also can help you attain oneness with the universe. Yoga also helps you achieve a healthier lifestyle because it facilitates weight loss, improves blood circulation, and boosts your flexibility.

As we shall see later in the book, different yoga techniques and Asanas demand for specific approaches to derive the expected benefits: unification of various aspects of the human spirit.

In this guide, we shall look at yoga from a varied perspective in a bid to help you derive the benefits offered by yoga.

Before we start discussing how to practice yoga, let us look at the benefits you stand to gain by practicing yoga. By looking at these benefits, you will feel inspired to start your 4-week Yoga challenge.

Why Practice Yoga?

Yoga uses various spiritual and physical exercises that bring many benefits to yoga yogis and yoginis (these are the respective names given to male and female yoga practitioners). For instance, yoga is useful for weight loss, building muscles, relieving stress, and strengthening the heart.

Regular practice can also help you achieve inner peace especially if you pair yoga with meditation. If you are looking for a refreshing leisure activity, yoga can still be an interesting exercise you can practice alone or with friends. Whatever reason you may have for wanting to become a yogi or yogini, yoga can deeply connect your mind, body, and spirit, which can help you experience your real self.

Let us detailedly discuss the various benefits yoga has for its practitioners:

1. Boosts Physical Fitness

Yoga uses various poses and stretches; what we call asanas. Research shows that holding asanas for at least 60 seconds can boost your posture and deadlift strength. Yoga can boost balance of strength onto your opposing muscle groups, and help you improve flexibility and range of motion.
The good thing is that yoga poses are simple and can fit everyone ranging from body builders, athletes, the obese, and members of either gender. When practiced properly, yoga reduces stress buildup in the muscles, relaxes you, and prevents possible workout injuries because it improves flexibility.

To benefit from yoga in terms of strength gains, elongated muscles, and boosting physical fitness, its best to adopt yoga as part of your regular workout program. For instance, doing yoga stretches before strength training allows the muscles to freely workout without actually shutting down in response to stretched tendons.

Better still, yoga aids movement through your full range of motion when hitting weights. With a full range of motion, you can build long and full-toned muscles or abs. Physical fitness experts are of the view that stretching yoga poses elongate the protective heath of connective tissues that cover muscles and its cells and repair worn out muscles.

The main reason why yoga energizes and strengthens muscle groups is the long deep breaths, something you have to do as you practice yoga asanas. These deep breaths supply oxygen to the muscles, and boost your ability to focus on workouts.

Yoga can fit into a busy or sedentary lifestyle. Further, some research shows that yoga can heal chronic pain such as migraines. Without much effort, a beginner yogi such as yourself can learn how to make informed health choices and practice specific yoga asanas and techniques aimed at improving your health. This lifestyle coaching can include various aspects like stress reduction, exercising, diet, mindfulness, and other relaxation techniques.

http://amzn.to/2bBlfTw

Here Is A Preview Of What You Can Learn From This Book.

- The Basics of Yoga
- Why Practice Yoga?
- How to Adopt Yoga in 4 weeks: A Three Step Approach
- 4-Week Step By Step Guide

Check out the rest of the book by searching for this title on Amazon website.

Check Out My Other Books

Below you'll find my other books that are popular on Amazon and Kindle as well.

- Chakras For Beginners: The 7 Chakras Guide On How to Balance your Energy Body through Chakra Healing
- Yoga: 4-Week Step By Step Guide for Yoga Beginners
- Buddhism for Beginners: 8 Step Guide to Finding Peace and Enlightenment in Your Life
- Ultimate Self-Mastery Bundle for Beginners 3 in 1 Bundle
- Mindfulness for Beginners: 21-Day Step By Step Guide to Relieve Stress and Find Peace in Your Everyday Life
- Happiness: A Little Guide To Self-Love And Positive Thinking

Made in the USA
Middletown, DE
17 November 2017